Grand-

Internet
Shopping

Linda Ingham

WILLOW
ISLAND
EDITIONS

Microsoft Internet Explorer is available free. It is
often included on computer magazine cover CDs
or it can be downloaded from
www.microsoft.com

Published by Willow Island Editions,
41 Water Lane, Middlestown,
Wakefield, WF4 4PX

www.willowisland.co.uk

ISBN 1-902467-08-6

CONTENTS

Introduction

Imagine the sort of day when the rain falls horizontally and your thermal underwear is tested to the limit ... the sort of day when you'd rather sit in front of the fire with your knitting and a cup of tea than leave the house to do the shopping, and you almost wish that the nice young man who rang the other day to offer you double glazing would phone back.

These are the perfect conditions for trying out an alternative – **Internet shopping**. It's possible to buy just about anything using your computer and placing your order 'online'.

With the help of my grandson, Simon, I hope to show you how you can do your supermarket shopping and buy gifts (and knitting yarn) without leaving home. All you need is a computer, with a connection to the Internet, and a credit or debit card.

Simon says – 'Most online shopping websites start with a home page which has links to other pages, like a catalogue. You add items to a **virtual shopping basket** and buy them all together at the end at a **virtual checkout**.'

Starting Out

Assuming that you
have a computer
with Internet access,
and you have
experimented with
sending e-mail messages and looking
up websites, you should be able to
shop online with only mild initial
anxiety.

You may wish to have the moral
support of someone who is familiar
with computers, or who has tried
Internet shopping already, when you
make your first attempt. The 'website
shops' you will use do try to make
things as straightforward as possible
and to lead you through the selection
and buying process logically, but some
do this more successfully than others.

In the same way that you knitted a pan-holder before attempting a lady's 2-ply cable-pattern twin set with picot edging and Swiss embroidery detail, it is a good idea to start with something simple. Ordering a 'trolley load' of groceries for the first time can be a slow process, but it becomes easier and quicker each time you do it.

Simon says – 'Grandma uses Microsoft's **Internet Explorer** for Internet access.'

Security Issues

You may be concerned about divulging details of your credit card online or about what to do if things go wrong. Fortunately, those who have developed Internet shopping sites have given a lot of thought to this too.

Most of the websites you are likely to visit on your online shopping trips use a **secure server** so that when you enter your details they are 'encrypted' or disguised in code. When using Internet Explorer you will see a little picture of a padlock at the bottom of the screen, indicating that the site is secure. Other sites don't take your card details online but ask you to phone them with the details afterwards.

Using a credit card for your online purchases limits your liability and protects your consumer rights in the same way that it does with transactions in shops or over the phone.

Details of delivery times, what to do about returning goods, if necessary, and how to request a refund should be displayed on the shopping website and you can check these before placing your order.

 Simon says – 'You could check out **www.which.net** for more information about shopping safely.'

The Supermarket

Online supermarket shopping facilities are constantly developing. Websites are improving, areas to which deliveries can be made are extending and new suppliers are offering Internet shopping.

Not all supermarkets will deliver to your area, but you can discover which ones are available to you by visiting the websites and entering your postcode in the appropriate box.

Websites to try are -
www.tesco.com
www.sainsbury.co.uk
www.iceland.co.uk

It would be possible to walk into a supermarket with your trolley or basket and to go up and down each aisle, perusing each item on the shelf and making your selection. Such a shopping trip might take hours, and the same applies if you shop this way on the Internet. Most people prefer to make a shopping list and to head for the shelf stocking a particular item.

Simon says – 'Some websites will remember what you have ordered in the past and make things easier by showing you a list of these items for you to order again if you wish.'

Armed with your shopping list, credit card and a cup of tea, you are now ready to go.........

1. Switch on your computer and launch **Internet Explorer** by clicking twice on the icon, using the mouse's left hand button. Click once on 'Connect' if this box appears and you will be shown your **home page.**

2. Enter the web address you want to visit in the **Address** box at the top of the page, starting **http://www**. For purposes of illustration, we will enter **http://www.tesco.com**

3. On the Tesco home page click once on 'Groceries online' at the left of the screen. There is then an option for existing customers to enter a password, but as a new customer you click once on 'register'. At this point there is a box where you can enter your postcode to check that deliveries are made to your area. If your area is not covered, try another supermarket website instead.

4. Type your name and address in the boxes indicated, using the **Tab** button on the keyboard to move to the next box.

Simon says – 'Before you start try to think up a password you'll be able to remember. It's easier than making one up on the spot if asked for it.'

5.   If you already have a Clubcard from the Tesco store, enter its number, otherwise click the box requesting one. This will allow any purchases you make in the store to be added to your 'favourites' shopping list when you're shopping online.

6.   Enter your e-mail address and a password which you'll be able to remember next time you do your Internet shopping. Click on 'sign in' to get to the 'welcome page'.

7.   You can decide when you would like your shopping to be delivered by clicking on 'click here to pre-view available delivery slots'. You will be shown a table of two hour slots and can select a day and time for delivery. If you wish, this can be chosen after you've done your shopping.

8. Return to the 'welcome page' by clicking on the 'welcome' tab at the top of the screen. Special offers will be shown on this page. You add an item to your shopping basket by clicking once with the left hand mouse button on 'add' and at any time, while doing your shopping, you can click on 'view my basket' to see a list of items you've selected already.

9. Across the top of the 'welcome page' are tabs with options such as 'browse', 'my order' and 'checkout'. Click on the one labelled 'shopping assistant', then click on 'express shopper'.

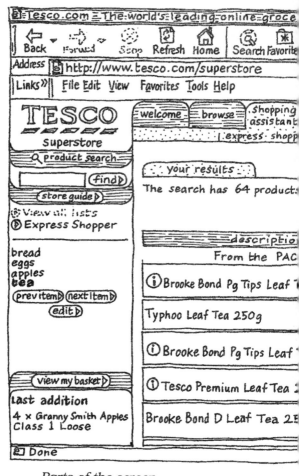

Tesco.com – The world's leading online groce

Back | Forward | Stop | Refresh | Home | Search Favorite

Address: http://www.tesco.com/superstore

Links» | File Edit View Favorites Tools Help

TESCO
superstore

Q product search

[   ] (find▷)
(store guide ▷)

▷ View all lists
▷ Express Shopper

bread
eggs
apples
tea
(prev item▷) (next item▷)
(edit▷)

(view my basket ▷)
Last addition
4 × Granny Smith Apples
Class 1 Loose

Done

welcome — browse — shopping assistant
express shopp

your results

The search has 64 products

description
From the PAC

ⓘ Brooke Bond Pg Tips Leaf T

Typhoo Leaf Tea 250g

ⓘ Brooke Bond Pg Tips Leaf

ⓘ Tesco Premium Leaf Tea

Brooke Bond D Leaf Tea 2E

Parts of the screen

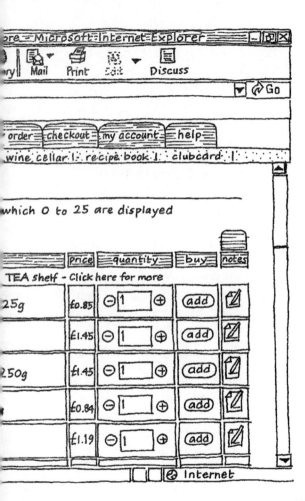

order   checkout   my account   help

wine cellar | recipe book | clubcard |

which 0 to 25 are displayed

	price	quantity	buy	notes
TEA shelf - Click here for more				
25g	£0.85	⊖ 1 ⊕	add	📝
	£1.45	⊖ 1 ⊕	add	📝
250g	£1.45	⊖ 1 ⊕	add	📝
	£0.84	⊖ 1 ⊕	add	📝
	£1.19	⊖ 1 ⊕	add	📝

Internet

17

10. Type a shopping list in the box
    e.g. 'bread, eggs, apples, tea, etc'
    and click once on 'go shopping'.
    You will be shown a list of all
    items containing the first word
    on your list, giving a description,
    price and quantity for each. You
    can change the quantity by

    clicking on ⊖ or ⊕

    and buy the item by clicking on
    the button labelled 'add'. Having
    selected your bread, click on
    'eggs' from your list at the left of
    the screen and select from the
    new list of items shown.

11. When you have found everything
    on your list click on the
    'checkout' tab near the top of the
    screen. Choose when you would
    like your shopping to be
    delivered if you haven't done so
    already then click on 'back' to
    return to the checkout.

12. Select whether you would like an appropriate substitute for any items out of stock.

13. Enter the payment details from your credit or debit card and you will be shown a 'guide price' to which a £5 delivery charge is added. If satisfied that your order is complete click on 'confirm my order' and your shopping is done.

14. Within a short time your order will be confirmed by e-mail and you can change the delivery time or cancel the whole order if necessary.

Knitting and Crafts

There are many websites relating to crafts and knitting yarns. Most of these are used as advertisements or catalogues for conventional shops and mail order outlets but an increasing number offer the opportunity to buy over the Internet. There will be a charge for delivery, and it's worth checking what this will be before you start shopping on a website.

Simon says – 'Even those websites which don't have the option to buy directly online may have an order form you can print out and send by post, with your payment, or you may be able to order by e-mail, then phone with your credit card details.'

Websites to try are -

www.knitting-yarn.co.uk
(for yarn, patterns and general
knitting supplies)

www.stitchability.co.uk
(for needlecraft kits and tapestry
wool)

www.colourway.co.uk
(for Rowan and Jaeger yarns)

Let's buy some wool.........

1. Following steps 1 and 2 on *Page 12* type in **http://www. knitting-yarn.co.uk.** The home page has various links which you can investigate. Click on 'what we do and how to contact us'. You will be shown details of how to order.

2. Down the left side of the screen is a list of options. Select 'Order Form' and either print out a copy of this (by clicking on the picture of a printer at the top of the screen) so that you can fill it in by hand, or **minimise** it by clicking on '-' at the top right hand corner of the screen.

3. Click on 'Site Map' to see the yarns available. If you click on a yarn from the list you will be shown a shade card with a Product Code and Wool Colour Code for each shade.

4. Having made your choice, enter
    the details on the order form.
    You can do this on the screen by
    clicking on the grey bar at the
    bottom of the screen which
    represents the minimised order
    form. The form will then be
    displayed on the screen. If you
    need to refer back to the shade
    card you can minimise the order
    form again and refer to it by
    clicking on the grey bar again.

5. You can browse through the site
    for other items and add these to
    your order.

6. When you have completed your
    selection fill in your name and
    address details on the order
    form and choose your method of
    payment.

7. Click on 'Send' at the foot of the
    order form and it will be
    submitted by e-mail.

Shopping Directories

If you want to buy a specific item you can use an online **shopping directory** to tell you at which Internet shopping sites it is available and to compare prices at different websites.

Suppose that we're looking for 'The Best of Glenn Miller' CD for a friend's birthday.

1. Following steps 1 and 2 on *Page 12* type in **http://uk.shopsmart. com** and click on 'Go'.

2. You will see the ShopSmart **home page**. Select 'First time visitor – click here' and you will be shown an explanation of the site.

3. Click on the arrow next to 'Back to About ShopSmart Index' and search for 'Music' (selected from a drop down menu by clicking on

the arrow at the right of the
'search' box, then clicking on
'Music').

4. Type 'Best of Glenn Miller' in the
    next search box and click on
    'Go'. You will be shown all the
    titles matching this search (I
    found that 10 similar titles were
    available) with a picture of the
    CD cover for each. There are
    options of selecting 'More info'
    and 'Compare prices' against
    each title.

5. Clicking on 'More info' lists the
    tracks on the CD and for some
    CDs you can select to hear
    samples of the tracks.

SEARCH RESULTS FOR Music "The Best of Glenn Miller"

Best Of Glenn Miller, The by Glenn Miller
This Release: n/a | Publisher: DBM
More info or Compare prices

6. Having decided on a particular CD, click on 'Compare prices'. This lists the online shops searched and the price of the CD at each, with postage and packing charges listed separately as well as a total price. (I found that the total price for my choice varied from £3.99 to £11.48 over 8 different shops).

7. After each entry in the 'Compare prices' table is a 'Go to Shop' link. If you click on this your screen will display the web page of the online store where you can buy the item.

Simon says – 'You may not want simply the cheapest option. Take into account estimated delivery times as well. These are shown too.'

Other shopping directories you could try are **www.kelkoo.com** and **www. mytaxi.co.uk**

When you have followed the instructions and shopped on the Internet a few times you should begin to feel confident about the process. Soon you'll be able to use the basic principles to find your way about websites and to shop online as easily as you might shop on the High Street.

Check that the shopping website is in this country. Sites ending in **.co.uk** will be in the UK, but some ending **.com** will be in other parts of the world.

You Might Like to Try

If you don't have a particular gift in mind, you might prefer to browse.

A useful website is **www.charitygifts. com** which puts the catalogues of several charities at your fingertips. The home page has links to the British Red Cross, Save the Children Fund, NSPCC, British Heart Foundation, Cancer Research Campaign and RSPCA, amongst others, and you can buy online.

For department store shopping there's **www.debenhams.com** and **www. johnlewis.com**

If you'd like to find out what special offers may be available at your local supermarkets, or other shops, try **www.priceoffers.co.uk**

The website **www.silversurfers.net** is worth a look for both grandmas and granddads. It has lots of links to items of interest, including stores.

Advertisements in the press or on TV and radio may give web addresses, with the opportunity to buy over the Internet.

 Simon says – 'Remember to check that a site is secure before entering your credit card details. Don't send your card details by e-mail.'

After Thoughts

Until you click on a button such as **send** or **confirm my order** you haven't committed yourself to buying anything and can leave the website without making a purchase.

Don't forget to close your Internet session when you've finished shopping. You can do this by clicking on the cross in the top right corner of the screen, then selecting Disconnect.

When online you are effectively making a phone call and this will be more expensive during the day. If you make your shopping list in advance, then do your online shopping in the evening or at weekends, you should reduce the cost. Internet shops are always open.

The costs of the Internet connection and delivery charges can be weighed against the savings in transport costs compared with ordinary shopping.

Think of the luxury of avoiding the crowds when doing your Christmas shopping from the comfort of your keyboard . . . and don't worry about the lack of personal contact with shop assistants because you'll become very well acquainted with the postman, as he delivers all your parcels!

If you should need a break from the Internet Shopping, you could always grab your purse and head to town for some serious retail therapy . . .